Faith FOR TOUGH TIMES

A 4-week course to help senior highers discover a Christian perspective on racism, prejudice, equality and personal rights

by Christine Yount

Group®

Loveland, Colorado

Responding to Injustice
Copyright © 1991 by Group Publishing, Inc.

First Printing

Credits
Edited by Stephen Parolini
Cover designed by Jill Christopher and DeWain Stoll
Interior designed by Judy Bienick and Jan Aufdemberge
Illustrations by Raymond Medici
Photo on p. 4 by Dale D. Gehman

ISBN 1-55945-214-5
Printed in the United States of America

CONTENTS

RESPONDING TO INJUSTICE

We live in a world of homelessness, poverty, war and pain. Too often when kids turn on the television or radio they hear about cities destroyed by earthquakes, countries invaded by armies, people slain in the streets or violent confrontations due to prejudice. Teenagers know about famine, and the mistreatment and oppression of helpless people. And, closer to home, they feel the pain of being rejected or overlooked.

Life just doesn't seem fair! And teenagers' sense of justice is strong. Kids want to know how to make a difference in the world.

But, although they have the desire, kids don't always know what to do. That's unfortunate. According to Search Institute's study on Christian education, service to less-fortunate people is one of the top three factors in teenagers' faith development.

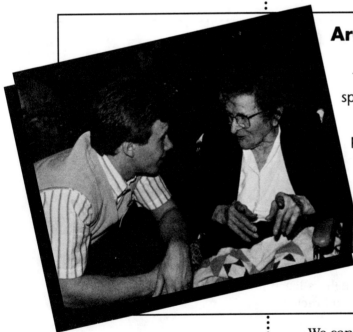

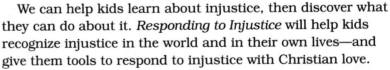

Are Kids Reaching Out?

The percentage of teenagers who say they spent three hours or more in the last month . . .

. . . helping friends or neighbors with problems—56%

. . . donating time helping children, youth or families—23%

. . . donating time helping people who are poor, hungry or sick—14%

. . . promoting social justice or peace—8%

We can help kids learn about injustice, then discover what they can do about it. *Responding to Injustice* will help kids recognize injustice in the world and in their own lives—and give them tools to respond to injustice with Christian love.

Kids will learn when it's appropriate to stand up for their rights—or for the rights of others. Teenagers will experience what it's like to feel prejudice—and commit to work toward eliminating prejudice around them. They'll explore why some people "play favorites," and how to respond to favoritism.

Teenagers will be reassured God is in control. They'll begin to understand causes of injustice. And, most important, kids will learn they *can* make a difference in the world.

So dive into *Responding to Injustice.* You and your students will be challenged to re-think your views on injustice in the world. And you'll be challenged to be a catalyst for making the world a better place.

During this course, your students will:
- learn the complex causes of injustice;
- discover ways to respond to injustice;
- read what the Bible says about people's rights;
- see how biblical characters experienced favoritism;
- learn how to confront favoritism;
- see how prejudices can hinder Christ's message; and
- answer God's challenge to bring justice to their relationships.

COURSE OBJECTIVES

HOW TO USE THIS COURSE

ACTIVE LEARNING

Think back on an important lesson you've learned in life. Did you learn it from reading about it? from hearing about it? from something you experienced? Chances are, the most important lessons you've learned came from something you experienced. That's what active learning is—learning by doing. And active learning is a key element in Group's Active Bible Curriculum.

Active learning leads students in doing things that help them understand important principles, messages and ideas. It's a discovery process that helps kids internalize what they learn.

Each lesson section in Group's Active Bible Curriculum plays an important part in active learning:

The **Opener** involves kids in the topic in fun and unusual ways.

The **Action and Reflection** includes an experience designed to evoke specific feelings in the students. This section also processes those feelings through "How did you feel?" questions and applies the message to situations kids face.

The **Bible Application** actively connects the topic with the Bible. It helps kids see how the Bible is relevant to the situations they face.

The **Commitment** helps students internalize the Bible's message and commit to make changes in their lives.

The **Closing** funnels the lesson's message into a time of creative reflection and prayer.

When you put all the sections together, you get a lesson that's fun to teach. And kids get messages they'll remember.

BEFORE THE 4-WEEK SESSION

● Read the introduction, the Course Objectives and This Course at a Glance.

● Decide how you'll publicize the course using the art on the Publicity Page (p. 9). Prepare fliers, newsletter articles and posters as needed.

● Look at the Bonus Ideas (p. 46) and decide which ones you'll use.

• Read the opening statements, Objectives and Bible Basis for the lesson. The Bible Basis shows how specific passages relate to senior highers today.

• Choose which Opener and Closing options to use. Each is appropriate for a different kind of group. The first option is often more active.

• Gather necessary supplies from This Lesson at a Glance.

• Read each section of the lesson. Adjust where necessary for your class size and meeting room.

• The approximate minutes listed give you an idea of how long each activity will take. Each lesson is designed to take 35 to 60 minutes. Shorten or lengthen activities as needed to fit your group.

• If you see you're going to have extra time, do an activity or two from the "If You Still Have Time" box or from the Bonus Ideas (p. 46).

• Dive into the activities with the kids. Don't be a spectator. The lesson will be more successful and rewarding to you and your students.

HELPFUL HINTS

• The answers given after discussion questions are responses your students *might* give. They aren't the only answers or the "right" answers. If needed, use them to spark discussion. Kids won't always say what you wish they'd say. That's why some of the responses given are negative or controversial. If someone responds negatively, don't be shocked. Accept the person, and use the opportunity to explore other angles of the issue.

THIS COURSE AT A GLANCE

Before you dive into the lessons, familiarize yourself with each lesson aim. Then read the scripture passages.
- Study them as a background to the lessons.
- Use them as a basis for your personal devotions.
- Think about how they relate to kids' circumstances today.

LESSON 1: THE HURTING WORLD

Lesson Aim: To help senior highers learn to respond to injustice with Christian love.

Bible Basis: Genesis 3:17-19 and Job 1:8-12

LESSON 2: I'VE GOT RIGHTS

Lesson Aim: To help senior highers identify the importance of rights and what to do when rights clash.

Bible Basis: Exodus 22:21-27; Matthew 5:38-42; and Philippians 2:3-5

LESSON 3: I GET NO RESPECT

Lesson Aim: To help senior highers cope with and confront favoritism.

Bible Basis: Genesis 25:24-28; 27:1-35; 37:3-5; and Jeremiah 31:3

LESSON 4: STEREOTYPING AND RACISM

Lesson Aim: To help senior highers learn how to confront the issues of stereotyping and racism.

Bible Basis: Isaiah 59:8-16a and Acts 10:1-35

PUBLICITY PAGE

Grab your senior highers' attention! Photocopy this page, then cut and paste the art of your choice in your church bulletin or newsletter to advertise this course on injustice. Or photocopy and use the ready-made flier as a bulletin insert. Permission to photocopy the clip art is granted for local church use.

Splash this art on posters, fliers or even postcards! Just add the vital details: the date and time the course begins and where you'll meet.

It's that simple.

RESPONDING TO
INJUSTICE

A 4-week high school course on prejudice, personal rights, favoritism and other injustices

Come to _____

On _____

At _____

Come learn how to respond in Christian love to injustice in the world!

THE HURTING WORLD

While many people enjoy the freedoms of going to church, voting for their favorite candidates or visiting local fast-food restaurants, others have never heard of these freedoms. Teenagers need to think about things that aren't fair about our world—and learn how, with God's help, they can right the wrongs.

LESSON AIM

To help senior highers learn how to respond to injustice with Christian love.

OBJECTIVES

Students will:
● experience injustice;
● learn the complex causes of injustice;
● discover ways to respond to injustice; and
● see how they can make a difference in the world.

BIBLE BASIS
GENESIS 3:17-19
JOB 1:8-12

Look up the following scriptures. Then read the background paragraphs to see how the passages relate to your senior highers.

In **Genesis 3:17-19**, Adam learns the consequences of sin.
Because of Adam and Eve's rebellion against God, sin entered the world and made it less than perfect. Injustice and all sorts of evils began to fill the world. People were destined for the rest of time to battle sin and a fallen world.
The causes of injustice are complex. Kids need to understand there are no easy answers to the question "why is there injustice?" But they can understand that one reason for injustice is the fall of humankind in the Garden of Eden.

In **Job 1:8-12**, God gives Satan permission to afflict Job.
Job is known for his unjust suffering. In this passage, God was pleased with his servant Job. But Satan told God Job

wouldn't be so blameless if God would let Satan afflict him.

Kids need to understand that Satan can also cause injustice. But kids can be encouraged to know Satan can't do anything without God's "permission." God is in control—even in the face of injustice. Because God is in control, kids can work together with him to right the injustices in the world.

THIS LESSON AT A GLANCE

Section	Minutes	What Students Will Do	Supplies
Opener (Option 1)	up to 5	**In the Bag**—Be given different kinds of goodie bags to experience injustice.	Bags, candy, fruit, rocks, scraps of paper, markers, paper
(Option 2)		**Have a Seat**—Experience the injustice of not having a place to sit down.	Masking tape
Action and Reflection	15 to 20	**World Council**—Participate in a mock United Nations discussion about injustice.	Paper, markers, "World Council" handout sections (p. 18)
Bible Application	10 to 15	**Why Is There Injustice?**—Learn the complex nature of injustice.	Bibles, pencils, "Why Injustice?" handouts (p. 19), newsprint, marker, tape
Commitment	10 to 15	**Bagged!**—Perform skits about ways to remedy injustice.	Bags filled with various items, "World Council" handout (p. 18)
Closing (Option 1)	up to 5	**World Relay**—Be encouraged to work for justice.	Marbles
(Option 2)		**World-Changer**—Pray for the needs of the world.	Globe, "I'm a World-Changer" ribbons (p. 17)

The Lesson

OPENER
(up to 5 minutes)

☐ OPTION 1: IN THE BAG

Before the lesson, prepare a "goodie" bag for each class member. In some of the bags, place candy, fruit and other edible items. Vary the number of items in each bag. In other bags, place rocks, scraps of paper and other useless items. Use a marker to number each bag. Then copy the numbers each onto separate slips of paper. Place the bags randomly on a table. Have kids sit so they can see the bags, but don't let them look inside the bags.

Say: **You'll each get to keep the ingredients of one bag. But first we'll decide who gets which bag.**

Go around the room and give kids each a slip of paper with a number on it. Tell kids they can trade numbers with someone else if they want to. Be sure kids don't look inside the bags. After a minute or so of trading, call time. Have kids each, one at a time, get their bag and reveal its contents to the rest of the class. Then have them form two groups based on whether the contents were good or bad.

Ask:

● **How did you feel when you saw what was in your bag?** (Disappointed; happy; relieved.)

● **How is getting a bag of rocks like being treated unjustly in life?** (It's not fair that we got rocks and others got food; it feels bad.)

Say: **Just as some people may've felt bad because they got a bag of rocks, some people in the world feel bad when they're treated unjustly. Today we're going to look at some of the injustices in the world.**

☐ OPTION 2: HAVE A SEAT

Use masking tape to divide the room in half. In one half of the room, place most of the chairs. In the other half, leave only enough chairs for one-fourth of your class members.

When kids arrive, have them count off by twos. Have the "ones" stand on the side of the room with the fewest chairs, and the "twos" stand on the side with the extra chairs. Don't let kids move the chairs across the dividing line.

Say: **At the count of three, you must each sit in a chair, but you must stay in your half of the room and you may not move any of the chairs.**

Count to three, then watch the kids find their seats.

Ask:

● **Is it fair that some people don't have chairs to sit in? Why or why not?** (No, we should each have a place to sit; yes, only the "best" people get to sit in chairs.)

Kids might tease about how the group with all the chairs is "better" than the other group. If so, use this opportunity to talk about how people sometimes think they're better because they have more than others. This discussion will lead nicely into the following questions about injustice.

Ask:

● **How does it feel to be on your side of the room?** (Fine, we have lots of space; uncomfortable, we don't all have chairs.)

● **How is this like the way people in less fortunate situations might feel as victims of injustice?** (They'd feel uncomfortable; the people with all the comforts are glad they're not like the people who don't have them.)

Kids on the side of the room with too few chairs may've

been creative and piled more than one person into each chair. If so, discuss how people who are victims of injustice often don't have the opportunities others have and must be creative with what they do have.

Say: **Today we'll be looking at injustices in the world and how we can respond to them in Christian love.**

ACTION AND REFLECTION
(15 to 20 minutes)

WORLD COUNCIL

Form six groups (a group can be one person). Assign each group one of the fictitious countries listed on the "World Council" handout (p. 18). If your class has fewer than six kids, use only as many countries as you have kids. Give groups each paper and markers.

Say: **For the next activity, you'll each be representing the country you've been assigned at a World Council meeting. You're meeting today to discuss the injustices in your countries and how they can be confronted. You'll each want the other countries to see your need as the most important need in the council. Only the country with the most serious injustices will be given support from the World Council to help solve the problems. Before the meeting, design a flag representing your country. Use the paper and markers to create your flags.**

Arrange chairs in a circle with members of each "country" sitting near one another. Have countries each tape their flag on a chair or table near them.

Say: **Take a couple minutes to plan how you'll present your plea for assistance to the World Council. Then each country will have two minutes to make its presentation. As you plan, be sure to think about how you might respond to other countries' claims.**

Distribute the "World Council" handout sections (p. 18) each to the appropriate team. After a couple minutes for countries to discuss their strategies, call time.

One at a time, have countries each present their case to the rest of the countries. Don't allow any talking during the presentations. After all the presentations, allow countries to react to what other countries said. Act as moderator and allow only one representative to speak at a time.

After a couple minutes, have a secret election to see which country's problem will be chosen as the one the World Council will deal with. Give kids each a sheet of paper and a pencil and have them write on the paper the name of the country they're voting for. Tell kids they can vote for their own countries. Collect and tally the votes to determine the winning country.

After the vote, ask:

● **How did you feel as you presented your case to the council? Explain.** (Frustrated, I didn't think they'd care about our country's problems; excited, I knew we could convince others about the seriousness of our problems.)

● **How easy was it to decide which country's injustices were most serious? Explain.** (It was very difficult, all the problems were serious; it was easy, some problems would be impossible to deal with.)

● **What can you learn from this activity about injustice?** (Injustice is difficult to overcome; people have different opinions about what injustice is; all injustice needs to be dealt with somehow.)

Say: **Of course all injustice is serious. But as we discovered in this activity, the questions "Why is there injustice?" and "What can we do about injustice?" aren't easy questions. We're going to try to answer them anyway, beginning with "Why is there injustice?"**

WHY IS THERE INJUSTICE?

Form groups of no more than four. Give groups each a "Why Injustice?" handout (p. 19), a Bible and a pencil. Have groups each follow the instructions, complete the handout and discuss the questions at the bottom of the handout.

Have groups each report back to the whole group.

Ask:

● **How easy was it to determine the reasons for injustice in each situation?** (It was very difficult because we didn't know the whole situation; it was difficult because there seemed to be lots of reasons; it was easy.)

Say: **Just as you may have struggled with completing the handout, we struggle with knowing the reasons injustice occurs. But one thing we know for sure, God is aware of the injustices that occur in our world.**

Ask:

● **If God is in control, why doesn't he do something about injustice?** (He lets us deal with it; he does, through his people; because he wants us to grow and learn from it.)

● **Does injustice in the world bring us closer to God? Why or why not?** (Yes, we learn to rely on God more; no, it separates us from God.)

Read aloud Ecclesiastes 7:13-14 and Romans 8:28.

Ask:

● **What do these verses tell us about God's role in our unjust world?** (God will work for good even when things look bad; God allows both good and bad to occur.)

● **Does God cause injustice to happen? Why or why not?** (Yes, since he's in charge and it does occur; no, we've messed up and are responsible for what happens.)

Say: **We don't know all the reasons injustice occurs in the world. But, as it says in 1 Corinthians 13:12a: "Now we see but a poor reflection as in a mirror; then we shall see face to face." We only see a small part of the picture. God sees the whole picture. We need to trust that God's in control and working his plan for good—even when we can't see the results.**

BIBLE APPLICATION
(10 to 15 minutes)

While we can't change our fallen world, we can help overcome injustice caused by ignorance and sin. Let's think of creative ways to fight injustice.

COMMITMENT
(10 to 15 minutes)

BAGGED!

Form groups of no more than six. Give groups each a bag with two or three items in it. Items you might use: a roll of toilet paper, a candy bar wrapper, a light bulb, a glove or a shoe. Vary the items in each bag so no two bags are alike.

Say: **To respond to injustice, we need to be creative. I'll assign each group a situation from the World Council activity. Your mission is to use the items in your bag to create a short skit that shows one way we can help fight the injustice described in your situation.**

Assign groups each one of the injustices from the "World Council" handout (p. 18); for example, poverty, disaster, racial discrimination, homelessness, war or political corruption.

Give groups five minutes to create their skits. Then have groups each present their skit to the whole class.

Ask:

● **How easy was it to use your items in your skit?** (Somewhat difficult; very easy.)

● **How was the creative use of the items like the way people must creatively deal with injustice?** (Victims of injustice must learn how to respond to injustice in creative ways; to fight injustice, we need to be resourceful.)

● **How can the creative ideas spark real-life solutions?** (We can act on the ideas we came up with; we can brainstorm more creative ideas based on the solutions in the skits.)

Have kids discuss which specific actions they can take individually and as a group to help fight injustice, such as raising money for charities that fight crime, abuse and prejudice; or raising awareness of specific injustices in the community. Help kids organize a task force or committee and begin planning at least one of the actions. Have kids commit to be involved in the action. Be sure to follow up on kids' decisions and help them put their plans into action.

Table Talk

The Table Talk activity in this course helps senior highers talk with their parents about injustice and choose ways to respond to it.

If you choose to use the Table Talk activity, this is a good time to show students the "Table Talk" handout (p. 20). Ask them to spend time with their parents completing it.

Before kids leave, give them each them each a "Table Talk" handout to take home, or tell them you'll be sending it to their parents.

Or use the Table Talk idea found in the Bonus Ideas (p. 47) for a meeting based on the handout.

☐ OPTION 1: WORLD RELAY

Have kids stand side by side in a line. Stand at one end of the line. Give a marble to the person next to you in line and complete this sentence: **(Name), you will bring justice to the world by your ...** Complete the sentence by describing a positive trait the person has that will enable him or her to make a difference in the world; for example, patience, concern for others, love, dynamic personality.

Then have that person pass the marble to the next person in line and complete the same sentence for the third person. After the second person passes the marble to the third person, pass a new marble to the second person. Continue this process until each person is holding a marble.

Say: **Each of these marbles represents the world we live in. Keep this marble as a reminder of all we can do to help the world be a better place.**

Have kids each carefully cup their marble in their hand as you close in prayer, thanking God for giving each person the ability to help fight injustice.

☐ OPTION 2: WORLD-CHANGER

Place a globe on a table. Have kids form a circle around the table. Have them each place one hand on the globe. If your group is too large to do this, have kids who can't reach the globe place their hands on the shoulders of others who are touching the globe. Spend a few moments in prayer, allowing kids to pray for specific needs in the world. Close by saying: **Thank you God for giving us the desire and ability to change the world and help overcome injustice.**

When you've finished praying, give kids each an "I'm a World–Changer" ribbon (in the margin) and say: **(Name), you're a world-changer because ...** For each person, describe an ability or character trait that makes him or her a world-changer; for example, you have love for others, you're good at being involved in world issues, you have a great desire to help.

CLOSING
(up to 5 minutes)

I'm a World-Changer!

Permission to photocopy this ribbon granted for local church use. Copyright © Group Publishing, Inc., Box 481, Loveland, CO 80539.

If You Still Have Time ...

Write to Your Rep—Get names and addresses of your local congressional representatives. Give kids each paper, a pen and a stamped envelope and have them write a letter expressing their concerns about specific injustices in the community and around the world.

Broken Body/Broken World—Scatter newspapers and news magazines on the floor. Have kids look through them to find reports of injustice around the world. Discuss the findings in groups of no more than five.

Then form a circle with kids sitting on the floor. Pass around a loaf of bread. Have kids each break off a piece of the bread and say a prayer for an injustice they read about.

WORLD COUNCIL

Photocopy and cut apart these sections.

Livinia

Situation: There are more than 10,000 refugees in this war-torn country. More than 200 civilians were recently gunned down in a church they thought was a safe haven.

Albankola

Situation: Christians are persecuted and imprisoned for their beliefs. It is believed certain high-level government officials are in charge of the anti-Christian actions.

Usurpasia

Situation: Homelessness and poverty plague the underprivileged classes. Each day, as people throw away millions of dollars in state lotteries, another hundred people lose their homes and move out into the streets.

Roomalia

Situation: Handicapped and mentally retarded children are institutionalized, neglected and given severely inadequate care.

South Tenovia

Situation: Racial discrimination and prejudice run rampant in this country. Every day people are killed in violent uprisings caused by segregation and unfair practices.

Durbania

Situation: People who refuse to grow marijuana or other illegal substances on their farms are being burned out, kidnapped or killed by drug lords who run the government.

WHY INJUSTICE?

Read each of the following situations and discuss why you think injustice occurred in each situation. Read the associated Bible verses to help you think about why some injustices might occur. Write your answers in the space provided. Then discuss the questions at the bottom of the handout.

● **Situation 1**—The people of Bogo-Bogo work their fields every year. They faithfully plant seeds in holes 6 feet deep and water them once a week. But there is rarely any growth. So the people suffer from famine in their land. Agricultural experts from other countries offer their services to the Bogo-Bogan government, but the officials won't accept any outside help. The officials are happy as long as there's food on their own tables.
   Read Isaiah 59:8 and Acts 17:22-28.
   Why is there injustice in Bogo-Bogo?

● **Situation 2**—Just when the people of Ragatan begin to rebuild their hurricane-wrecked homes, their country is hit with a major earthquake. Thousands of people are killed in the second major disaster in less than four months.
   Read Genesis 3:17-19.
   Why is there injustice in Ragatan?

● **Situation 3**—A luxury liner in the Pacific Ocean is attacked by terrorists. When the demands for millions of dollars in ransom aren't met, the terrorists blow up the ship, killing all its passengers.
   Read Romans 5:12; 1 Corinthians 10:24; and Titus 3:3-5.
   Why is there injustice on the luxury liner?

Discussion questions:
● How do you feel when you hear about injustice in the world?
● Is it easy to understand why injustice occurs? Why or why not?
● How does knowing the reasons for injustice make it easier or harder to deal with?
● Could ignorance (Acts 9:1-22); sin (Titus 3:3-5); the fallen world (Genesis 3:17-19); and Satan (Job 1:8-12) be reasons for injustice in the world? Read the associated scriptures and discuss how each item listed could be a reason for injustice.

Table Talk

To the Parent: We're involved in a senior high course at church called *Responding to Injustice*. Students are exploring a Christian perspective on injustice in the world. We'd like you and your teenager to spend some time discussing this important topic together. Use this "Table Talk" page to help you do that.

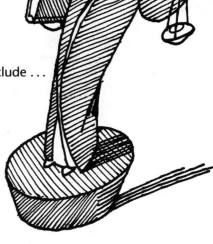

Parent
Complete the following sentences:
- When I was a teenager, the injustices that bothered me most were . . .
- Some things I've done to help right the wrongs of injustice are . . .
- A time I felt I was treated unfairly was . . .
- When I was a teenager, the most important world issues were . . .

Senior higher
- The injustices that bother me most are . . .
- Some things I'd like to do to help right the wrongs of injustice include . . .
- When I see friends at school treated unfairly, I . . .
- The most important world issues today are . . .

Parent and senior higher
Complete the following sentences:
- When I hear the word "injustice" I think of . . .
- Racism and prejudice make me feel . . .
- When people play favorites, I feel . . .
- God's role in the midst of all the injustice in the world is . . .
- The Bible can help me deal with injustice by . . .

Talk about injustices you'd like to see changed. Then brainstorm practical ways you can help right those injustices. Write out your ideas and decide when and how you'll take action on them.

After you've determined your plan, ask for support from other families to carry out your tasks. Then be sure to evaluate the effectiveness of your actions.

Together read Psalm 31:24; Isaiah 54:10; and Matthew 12:36. Discuss how these passages might help people wronged by injustice. Then think of one way you can send a message of hope to people who may not have much hope.

Pray daily for the next month that God will strengthen people to right the wrongs of injustice in the world.

I'VE GOT RIGHTS

"It's mine!" "Give it to me!" "I'm telling!"
From the time they're toddlers, kids understand they have rights. Their sense of justice is deeply ingrained, and it's easily ignited when someone violates their rights.

When toddlers become teenagers, the nursery scene changes—but only slightly. "Hey, watch it! That's my car." "How come she gets to stay out late and I don't?" "Leave me alone; I'm watching television."

But when we become Christians, God challenges us to trust him to defend our rights. We learn that our rights are really privileges. Teenagers need to be able to identify rights worth fighting for and rights they may need to give up.

To help senior highers identify the importance of rights and what to do when rights clash.

LESSON AIM

Students will:
● **learn what their rights are;**
● **experience rights that clash;**
● **discover what the Bible says about people's rights; and**
● **understand when to give up rights.**

OBJECTIVES

Look up the following scriptures. Then read the background paragraphs to see how the passages relate to your senior highers.

In **Exodus 22:21-27**, God defends the rights of his people.
In these verses, God promises that if anyone wrongs or oppresses a neighbor, he will defend the oppressed person. If anyone cries out from being afflicted, God will hear and bring about justice in his time.

BIBLE BASIS
EXODUS 22:21-27
MATTHEW 5:38-42
PHILIPPIANS 2:3-5

LESSON TWO ● 21

Christians can trust that God is looking out for their rights. Teenagers can learn not to walk all over others in the name of rights and, instead, count on God to help them defend important rights.

In **Matthew 5:38-42** and **Philippians 2:3-5**, God issues a challenge to Christians to give up their rights.

Although God defends our rights, he encourages us to let go of them. When we do, we learn to trust God and grow in Christlikeness. God also asks us to defend others' rights unselfishly.

Holding on to rights out of selfishness and pride doesn't reveal to the world who Christ is. By yielding rights to others, or fighting for others' rights, Christian teenagers can open a window so others can see what Christ is really like.

THIS LESSON AT A GLANCE

Section	Minutes	What Students Will Do	Supplies
Opener (Option 1)	5 to 10	**Signature Hunt**—Find people who have exercised certain rights.	"Signature Hunt" hand-outs (p. 28), pencils
(Option 2)		**Tower Rights**—Build a tower of cards.	3×5 cards, marker
Action and Reflection	10 to 15	**Exercising Rights**—Experience rights that clash.	Masking tape, "My Rights" handout (p. 29), cookies, punch, punch bowl, cups, tape player, cassette
Bible Application	10 to 15	**Yield and Assist**—Discuss giving up rights and standing up for others' rights.	Bible, "My Rights" hand-out sections (p. 29), paper, pencils
Commitment	10 to 15	**You Have the Right**—Determine rights they'll give up and rights they'll fight for.	Newsprint, marker, tape, paper, pencils
Closing (Option 1)	up to 5	**No More Thorns**—Pass around a rose and pray to know when to give up rights.	Rose, Bible
(Option 2)		**Right Posters**—Create posters describing rights they're willing to give up.	Posterboard, markers

The Lesson

☐ OPTION 1: SIGNATURE HUNT

When kids arrive, give each a "Signature Hunt" handout (p. 28) and a pencil. Have kids find people in the classroom (and in other classrooms, if you've notified them ahead of time) who can sign the squares on the handout. Depending on the size of your class, you may decide to allow kids to collect up to two or three signatures from any one person.

Allow five minutes for kids to collect signatures. Then form a circle.

Ask:

● **How easy was it to collect these signatures? Explain.** (Easy, these things are fairly common; not very easy, people didn't want to sign my paper.)

● **What's similar about all these items?** (They're all rights we have.)

Say: **Each item on your handout represents a right we have. But not everyone is afforded these rights. And sometimes rights conflict with each other. Today we'll be discussing a Christian perspective on rights. And we'll discover how our rights are really privileges.**

☐ OPTION 2: TOWER RIGHTS

Have kids brainstorm rights people have; for example, the right to live, the right to have privacy, the right to vote, the right to choose a religion. Have a volunteer write the rights each on a separate 3×5 card. Be sure kids brainstorm at least twenty rights. Encourage kids to be specific.

Have kids vote on the three rights they think are most important. Place the cards in order on a table. Then have a volunteer or two use the cards with the most important rights written on them to form the base of a "card tower." Then encourage kids to work together to build the tower as tall as possible using the rest of the cards.

Say: **This tower represents many of the rights we have. But some people don't have all these rights.** (Carefully take one or two cards off the top of the tower. Try not to topple the tower.) **And sometimes, our rights clash with other people's rights.** (Pull a card from the base of the tower. It will likely fall down.)

Ask:

● **How important are rights? Explain.** (Very important, they allow us freedom to do what we want; not very important, people don't exercise their rights very often.)

● **Did you agree with the rights chosen to be the foundation of the tower? Why or why not?** (Yes, I think they were the most important rights; no, I think other rights should've been first.)

● **How is what happened to the tower when I took away rights like what might happen if people didn't have rights?** (Our society would fall apart; people would be depressed.)

Say: **Today we'll examine a Christian perspective on rights. And we'll discover how our rights are really privileges.**

Table Talk Follow-Up

If you sent the "Table Talk" handout (p. 20) to parents last week, discuss students' reactions to the activity. Ask volunteers to share what they learned from the discussion with their parents.

ACTION AND REFLECTION
(10 to 15 minutes)

EXERCISING RIGHTS

With masking tape, make two lines on the floor that intersect in the center, dividing the room into four quadrants. Designate each quadrant as A, B, C or D. Put cookies in quadrant A; punch in quadrant B; a tape player and cassette in quadrant C; and chairs in quadrant D.

Form four groups, and put a different group in each quadrant. (A group can be one person.) Give groups each the appropriate "My Rights" handout section (p. 29).

Say: **For the next six minutes, you have only the rights listed on your card. Don't worry about other groups' rights—just exercise your own. Follow the rules on your handout, and do your best to enjoy some cookies, punch and music during this time.**

Give groups six minutes to exercise their rights—or protest the lack of certain rights. If groups try to exercise rights they don't have, tell the whole group what they're doing and take away more of their rights for breaking the law.

After six minutes, have groups each sit in their quadrant. Ask:

● **How did you feel about your rights?** (I didn't like our group's rights; we didn't have enough rights; we had plenty of rights.)

● **How did you feel when you had a right but couldn't exercise it? Explain.** (Frustrated, I wanted to have some punch but couldn't cross the line to get it; fine, I had the right to play loud music but didn't care to.)

● **How did you feel when your rights clashed with someone else's? Explain.** (Angry, I wanted to exercise my right of peace and quiet but another group was playing loud music; it was fun, I enjoy the challenge of clashing with someone else.)

● **Which group do you think had the most rights? the least rights?**

● **Were you tempted to cheat and exercise a right you didn't have? Why or why not?** (Yes, I didn't think it was fair that other people could have food and punch; no, I followed the rules even though I wished I'd had more rights.)

Give cookies and punch to the groups that didn't already have some. Continue the discussion by asking:

● **How was this activity like what happens with rights in the real world?** (Some people seem to have more rights than others; people's rights often clash.)

Have kids describe situations in real life that are similar to the ones kids experienced in this activity; for example, "Homeless people don't seem to have the right to shelter" or "Rich people sometimes overrule the rights of poor people."

Ask:

● **What's our responsibility as Christians when it comes to people's rights?** (We should stand up for our rights; we should help people who don't have as many rights; we should give up our rights when they clash with others' rights.)

● **Are the rights we've been talking about really more like privileges? Why or why not?** (Yes, we've been given the opportunities for freedom of speech and other freedoms, not because we deserve them but as a gift; no, we really deserve these rights.)

Say: **Until now, we've been talking about personal rights. Yet maybe we should think about these rights as privileges. We don't have rights because we deserve them, but because God has granted them to us. Let's look at what the Bible has to say about rights.**

YIELD AND ASSIST

Have kids remain in their quadrant groups. Read aloud Exodus 22:21-27; Matthew 5:38-42; and Philippians 2:3-5.

Ask:

● **What principles do these verses give about rights?** (We need to give up our rights sometimes; we need to think of others' needs before our own; God will defend our rights.)

● **According to these verses, why is it sometimes important to give up a right or privilege?** (Because others' needs are more important; because we're supposed to be humble.)

● **Is it easy to give up a privilege you have? Why or why not?** (No, I like having certain freedoms and would miss them; yes, if God wants me to give up a privilege, I'll gladly do it.)

Give groups each a sheet of paper and a pencil. Have groups each discuss which right on their "My Rights" handout section from the previous activity they'd be willing to give to another group. Then have them decide which group they'd give the right to. Have them each write it on paper. For example, group D might decide to give the right to sit in chairs to group C.

Have groups each present their paper to the appropriate group. Then have groups act out their new rights for a minute or two.

Ask:

● **How difficult was it to give up your rights?** (Very difficult, we didn't have many to begin with; easy, others needed this right more than we did.)

● **How is giving up one of your rights in this activity like following the principles outlined in the Bible verses?** (We had to think of others' needs ahead of ours; it's different, we gave what we didn't need instead of what others needed.)

● **When should we yield our rights to others?** (When we're simply being stubborn about our rights; when holding on to our rights hurts others.)

Remove the tape that separated the quadrants. Have kids go around and shake hands with each other. Then form a circle.

Say: **The Bible gives us clear messages concerning rights. It tells us God will defend our rights. And it tells us we may have to give up rights from time to time, and that we should look out for others' rights. How we respond to these messages is what's most important.**

COMMITMENT
(10 to 15 minutes)

YOU HAVE THE RIGHT

Have kids brainstorm rights people have, such as the right to watch what you want on television and the right to eat whatever you choose. Think of these items in terms of relationships with friends, family members and strangers. Write these rights on a sheet of newsprint and tape it to a wall. Then give kids each a sheet of paper and a pencil. Have kids each draw a vertical line down the center of their paper and title the left column "Willing to Give" and the right column "Worth Fighting For."

Say: **In the column on the left, list rights or privileges from the newsprint list you'd be willing to give up if they clashed with someone else's rights. In the other column, list rights from the newsprint list you'd be willing to "fight" for because you think they're especially important. As you write your lists, think about what Jesus would do in each situation.**

Allow five minutes for kids to complete their lists. Then form groups of no more than three, and have groups discuss their lists. Encourage kids to discuss specific ways they can follow through with the items on their lists.

After a couple minutes of discussion, form a circle and ask:

● **What did you learn in your group discussion?** (We each have strong feelings about certain rights; we each believe different rights are important.)

Have kids each tell one way they'll use what they've learned about rights; for example, "I'll be more willing to let my brother watch the shows he wants even though I was there first" or

"I'll write to my congressional representative and express my concern about elderly or disabled people not having the rights I have."

☐ OPTION 1: NO MORE THORNS

Hold up a rose.

Say: **Rights are a wonderful thing to have. But like this rose, rights sometimes have thorns. One thorn is our own inflexibility with rights; and another is that people are often denied basic rights. In many countries, people's rights are severely limited. I'm going to pass this rose around the circle. When you hold the rose, silently pray for wisdom to know when to give up rights. Or pray that people with limited rights might gain new rights. Then pass the rose to your left.**

Say your prayer, then pass the rose to your left. When it reaches you again, read aloud 2 Corinthians 2:15. Give a rose petal to each person as you say: **(Name), you are the fragrance of Christ. In all your conflicts and endeavors, remember to act as Christ would—being patient, kind and fair and speaking up for the oppressed.**

☐ OPTION 2: RIGHT POSTERS

Form groups of no more than four. Give groups each posterboard and markers. Have groups each design a simple poster that describes a time it's appropriate to give up a right or a privilege.

Have groups each present their poster to the other groups. Have kids each say one thing they like about the posters; for example, "I like the way you described the right you'd give up" or "I like the way you illustrated your poster." Then close in prayer, thanking God for giving us the rights we have and for defending our rights.

CLOSING
(up to 5 minutes)

If You Still Have Time . . .

Defender—Form groups of no more than five. Assign groups each one of the following topics: freedom of speech, right to live wherever you want, freedom of worship, right to eat food. Have groups each brainstorm ways God defends these rights and ways they can help defend these rights for less-fortunate people. Discuss times people may have to give up these rights.

Comic-Strip Completion—Tape six or seven sheets of paper side by side on a wall. Give kids markers and have them work together to create a comic strip that depicts some aspect of personal rights. Kids might show someone standing up for another person's rights; for example, someone standing up for the rights of handicapped people by visiting businesses and asking them to build wheelchair ramps or provide handicapped parking.

Signature Hunt

See how many signatures you can get on this handout. Find someone who . . .

has spoken out for a cause (list the cause).	has watched a TV show about lawyers.	is currently breathing.	can tell what it means to "plead the Fifth."	can say the pledge of allegiance.
has worshiped in church.	has a lock on the front door of his or her house.	has told a friend about Christ.	has a friend who's a police officer.	voted in the last national election.
knows the name of someone who's fought for people's rights.	can tell what the First Amendment rights are.	can recite his or her social security number from memory.	has never had his or her house searched by police.	has ever had a part-time job.
has read a newspaper.	can recite part of the Miranda rights.	can finish the phrase: innocent until . . .	has prayed in public.	owns a Bible.

MY RIGHTS

Photocopy this handout and cut apart the sections. Give one section to each group.

My Rights—Group A

You have:

- the right to eat.
- the right to enjoy peace and quiet.
- the right to cross into other quadrants.

You don't have:

- the right to play loud music.
- the right to drink punch.
- the right to sit in chairs.
- the right to protest your situation.

My Rights—Group B

You have:

- the right to eat.
- the right to enjoy peace and quiet.
- the right to cross into other quadrants.
- the right to drink punch.
- the right to protest your situation.

You don't have:

- the right to sit in chairs.
- the right to play loud music.

My Rights—Group C

You have:

- the right to play loud music.
- the right to eat.
- the right to protest your situation.

You don't have:

- the right to sit in chairs.
- the right to cross into other quadrants.
- the right to drink punch.

My Rights—Group D

You have:

- the right to drink punch.
- the right to sit in chairs.
- the right to play loud music.

You don't have:

- the right to cross into other quadrants.
- the right to eat.
- the right to protest your situation.

LESSON 3

I GET NO RESPECT

Everyone has felt the sting of not being someone's favorite—not being the teacher's pet, Sally's best friend, first pick for the volleyball team or homecoming king or queen. But kids can be encouraged by knowing they're each God's favorite.

LESSON AIM

To help senior highers cope with and confront favoritism.

OBJECTIVES

Students will:
- **experience favoritism;**
- **see how biblical characters experienced favoritism;**
- **learn how to confront favoritism; and**
- **learn they're each God's favorite.**

BIBLE BASIS

GENESIS 25:24-28; 27:1-35; 37:3-5
JEREMIAH 31:3

Look up the following scriptures. Then read the background paragraphs to see how the passages relate to your senior highers.

In **Genesis 25:24-28; 27:1-35; and 37:3-5**, sibling rivalry is complicated by parents' favoritism.

Joseph's brothers grew to hate him so much they sold him into slavery. And Jacob and Esau's relationship with their parents led to deception.

Teenagers, too, are confronted with issues of favoritism at home, school and even church. But kids can learn positive ways to confront the injustice of favoritism.

In **Jeremiah 31:3**, God assures his people he loves them.

God loves us with an everlasting love—an unconditional love that has no favorites.

Too often, kids' self-esteem is shattered when someone else gets the attention they wanted. When kids feel like they're second best, they can rely on the message of this passage—that God cherishes them and loves them as favorites.

Section	Minutes	What Students Will Do	Supplies
Opener (Option 1)	5 to 10	**Above the Rest**—Experience what it's like to be victims of favoritism.	Crumpled papers, trash bags, candy bar
(Option 2)		**The Best Test**—Create posters and experience favoritism.	Posterboard, markers
Action and Reflection	10 to 15	**Respect Bowl**—Play a game to experience favoritism.	Doughnuts, napkins, "Respect Bowl" handout (p. 36), "Game Cards and Parts" handout (p. 37), bowl
Bible Application	10 to 15	**Favoritism, Old and New**—Act out modern versions of Bible stories.	Bibles
Commitment	10 to 15	**No More Favorites**—Commit to confront favoritism and to watch out for their own favoritism.	Paper, pencils
Closing (Option 1)	up to 5	**God's Favorite**—Make "favorite" symbols for each other.	Modeling clay, straws, toothpicks
(Option 2)		**God's Favorite: The Sequel**—See that they are each God's favorite.	Cross, candle, matches

NOTE: Before you lead this lesson, you'll need to evaluate if you play favorites with people in your class. Be honest with yourself. Do you usually call on the same people to help out? Do you spend more time outside of class talking with particular kids? This lesson may bring out feelings in kids who've felt slighted by you. Be prepared to say "I'm sorry" if you need to. This will be an eye-opening lesson for you, as well as your students.

The Lesson

☐ OPTION 1: ABOVE THE REST

Before the class, crumple up some papers and spread them around the room. Make the floor as messy as possible so kids will have a few minutes of cleaning to do when they arrive.

As kids arrive, tell them to clean the room before the class begins. Give kids trash bags and let them get started. Before the cleaning gets going, have one person sit by you. Tell everyone that this person doesn't need to help with the cleaning. Be careful not to choose someone you might truly consider a favorite student.

While other kids continue to clean, pull out a candy bar and share it with your partner. Toss the wrapper onto the

OPENER
(5 to 10 minutes)

floor for others to pick up. Keep pushing kids to get the cleaning done.

After the room is clean, have everyone sit down.

Ask:

● **How did you feel about having to clean the room?** (Angry; upset; fine.)

● **How did you feel when I singled one person out who didn't have to help? Explain.** (Angry, it wasn't fair; upset, you were playing favorites.)

Tell kids you singled out this person simply to make the point you'll be discussing.

Ask:

● **How is this like when teachers, parents and even friends play favorites?** (It makes others feel left out or unimportant; it hurts; it's not fair.)

Say: **Today we're going to talk about when people have favorites. And we'll see how we can deal with favoritism.**

☐ OPTION 2: THE BEST TEST

Tell kids they're going to make posters to advertise next week's lesson on stereotyping and racism. Tell kids they'll have just five minutes to create their posters. Encourage kids to make posters that would draw kids to the class.

Give kids each posterboard and markers. After five minutes, have kids stop and present their posters. Then choose one poster you think is great. Go overboard about how wonderful it is and how you're sure it's the most creative poster you've seen. Say nothing about any of the other posters. Place the favored poster at the front of the room and place the others in a pile face down on the floor.

Form a circle and ask:

● **How does it make you feel that I singled out one poster and said nothing about the other posters?** (I feel bad; I'm disappointed; I feel like I wasted my time.)

Let kids know you only singled out a particular poster for the sake of this activity. Hang all the posters on the wall for everyone to see.

Ask:

● **How is the way I singled out one poster like the way some people play favorites?** (Some people ignore everyone except their favorite people; some people ignore others' ideas.)

Say: **Today we're going to look at the injustice of favoritism.**

RESPECT BOWL

If your group is larger than 10, create groups of no more than 10 and follow the instructions below for each group. You'll need a volunteer to be the "Rulemaster."

For each group of 10, photocopy the "Respect Bowl" game board (p. 36). Also photocopy the "Game Cards and Parts"

**ACTION AND
REFLECTION**

(10 to 15 minutes)

handout (p. 37), and cut apart the Respect Cards, Disrespect Cards and Number Slips. Place the Respect Cards and Disrespect Cards face down in separate piles. Fold the Number Slips each in half and place them in a bowl.

Have each group sit in a circle on the floor. Place the "Respect Bowl" game board, Respect Cards, Disrespect Cards and Number-Slips bowl in the center of the circle. Place one doughnut on a napkin in front of each person. Tell kids not to eat the doughnuts; they're part of the game. Have kids each find a playing piece; for example, a coin, an earring, a key, a paper wad or a paper clip.

Say: **We're going to play the Respect Bowl game. Each person will, in turn, pick up one Number Slip from the bowl and move his or her playing piece the appropriate number of spaces on the board. If someone lands on a Respect or Disrespect space, he or she must pick up the appropriate card and do what it says. The game is over when someone goes around the board once and reaches "start." The only other rule is that the Rulemaster may change the rules at any time. If you don't like a rule the Rulemaster has changed, you may protest—but the Rulemaster may or may not change his or her mind.**

Have the Rulemaster choose two or three game-players to give special favors to. Have the Rulemaster change the rules for those people to make sure they always get the best possible moves. For example, if a favorite person lands on a Disrespect space, the Rulemaster may tell that player to draw a Respect Card instead. Or, if a player picks a "one" Number Slip, the Rulemaster may tell the player to move five spaces instead. Other players will probably complain. Have the Rulemaster give in to their complaints at least once during the game and reverse a decision. But be sure the favorite players continue to get preferential treatment.

Have the person who's wearing the most colorful shoes go first. As the Respect Cards and Disrespect Cards are drawn, have players replace them at the bottom of each pile. During the game, have kids move the doughnuts around with the napkins. After someone wins the game, tell kids they can eat the doughnuts.

Ask:

● **How did you feel when the Rulemaster made it easier for some players to win?** (It was unfair; angry; upset.)

● **How did you feel when the Rulemaster listened to your complaints and reversed a decision? Explain.** (Great, I was glad the Rulemaster listened; good, it made me feel like my input was important.)

● **Do people always know they're playing favorites? Why or why not?** (Yes, they usually do it to make others feel bad; no, they don't usually think about it.)

● **How do you feel when people "play favorites?"** (Angry; upset; it doesn't bother me.)

● **Why do people show favoritism?** (They like the way

certain people look or think; they don't know any better.)

● **How is showing favoritism different from having "best friends"?** (Favoritism excludes others; it's not different.)

Say: **Favoritism hurts relationships. Well, favoritism isn't new. Next we'll take a look at some Bible stories that show how people played favorites.**

FAVORITISM, OLD AND NEW

Form two groups. Assign one of the following passages to each group: Genesis 25:24-28, 27:1-35; or Genesis 37:3-5, 18-28. Have groups each read their verses and create a skit based on those verses. Tell groups their skits should be modern-day versions of the stories. For example, the Genesis 37 skit could be about a brother who's given more freedom than his brothers and sisters, and how the favored brother is picked on by his brothers and sisters.

Have groups each present their skit. After each skit, have kids briefly discuss how they felt as participants in the skit. Then discuss how these biblical situations are similar to favoritism kids experience today.

Ask:

● **How would you have felt as Joseph? Joseph's brothers? Jacob? Esau?**

● **What can we do to help friends, family members or teachers keep from playing favorites?** (Confront them about the issue; tell them how you feel.)

Have someone read aloud Jeremiah 31:3.

Ask:

● **Does God have favorite people? Why or why not?** (Yes, Christians are his favorites; no, he loves everyone the same.)

● **How does it feel to be loved by God?** (Great; fantastic.)

Say: **God's love makes each one of us his favorite. But some people aren't fair about the way they treat others. We can confront favoritism, but we can't always change the way people think or act toward others. When we feel less than favored by friends, family or others we can always know we're still God's favorites.**

NO MORE FAVORITES

Give kids each a sheet of paper and a pencil. Have kids think of times they've been hurt by others because of favoritism. Have them each write a letter to one person who hurt them, explaining how they felt and gently suggesting ways to change the situation. For example, someone might write: "Dear Jim, I feel hurt that you didn't invite me to your graduation party. I know we don't always get along, but I care for you and I want to be your friend." Tell kids they'll each share their letter with a partner but won't have to reveal who they're writing to. Explain that they won't actually send the letters.

Allow three or four minutes for kids to silently write their

BIBLE APPLICATION
(10 to 15 minutes)

COMMITMENT
(10 to 15 minutes)

letters. Then have kids each find a partner they don't usually talk with. Have partners each read their letters aloud and talk about ways to confront the favoritism in each situation.

Then have partners each think about times they've shown favoritism and excluded others. Have kids each write on the back of their papers another letter—apologizing to someone they hurt by their actions.

Form a circle. Have kids each tell one thing they'll do to deal with favoritism in the future; for example, "I'll confront people who play favorites and tell them how I feel" or "I'll rely on God's love when others play favorites." Have kids close their eyes and reflect on Micah 6:8 as you read it aloud.

☐ OPTION 1: GOD'S FAVORITE

Give kids each some modeling clay, straws and toothpicks. Have them each create a symbol representing how God sees each person as a favorite. For example, kids might create sculptures such as "number one" signs, trophies or hearts.

Form a circle. Have kids each describe their sculpture and then present it to the person on their left. Have kids each complete the following sentence as they present their sculpture: "You're God's favorite because ..." Kids might complete the sentence by describing a positive trait the person has such as friendliness, a caring attitude or patience.

Close with prayer, asking God to help each person avoid playing favorites.

☐ OPTION 2: GOD'S FAVORITE: THE SEQUEL

Place a cross and a candle on the floor. Have kids sit on the floor in a circle around the cross and candle. Light the candle and turn off the lights. Have kids hold hands. One at a time, have kids each say to the person on their right: **Jesus died for you. You're God's favorite.**

Then close in prayer, thanking God for loving each person and asking for God's help in dealing with favoritism.

CLOSING
(up to 5 minutes)

If You Still Have Time ...

New Favorites—Have kids each think of someone at school or home who probably hasn't felt like a favorite to anyone recently. Have kids brainstorm creative ways to show this person they care about him or her. Then have kids commit to use their ideas to show their new favorites how important they are.

My Favorite Things—Give kids each a sheet of paper and a pencil. Have kids each list their name, favorite food and favorite musical artist or group. Collect the papers and shuffle them. Then read the papers aloud (except for the names) and have kids guess who wrote each one. Afterward, discuss how it's okay to have favorite things, but often hurtful or unjust to have favorite people.

GAME CARDS AND PARTS

Number Slips

1 2 3 4

Disrespect Cards

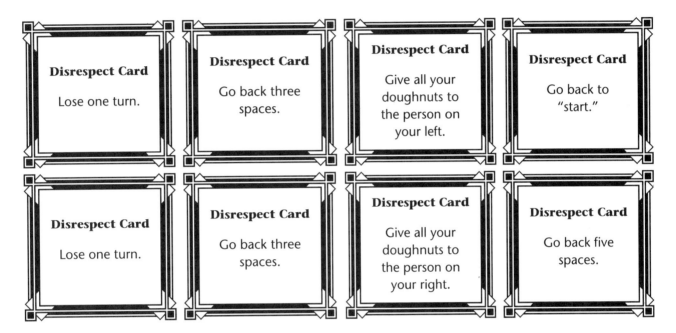

Disrespect Card

Lose one turn.

Disrespect Card

Go back three spaces.

Disrespect Card

Give all your doughnuts to the person on your left.

Disrespect Card

Go back to "start."

Disrespect Card

Lose one turn.

Disrespect Card

Go back three spaces.

Disrespect Card

Give all your doughnuts to the person on your right.

Disrespect Card

Go back five spaces.

Respect Cards

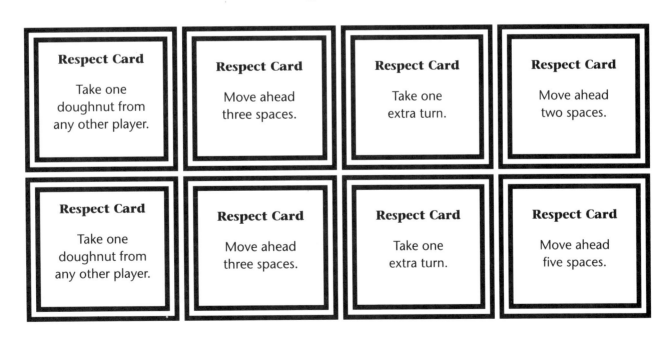

Respect Card

Take one doughnut from any other player.

Respect Card

Move ahead three spaces.

Respect Card

Take one extra turn.

Respect Card

Move ahead two spaces.

Respect Card

Take one doughnut from any other player.

Respect Card

Move ahead three spaces.

Respect Card

Take one extra turn.

Respect Card

Move ahead five spaces.

STEREOTYPING AND RACISM

Teenagers deal with the issues of stereotyping and racism daily. Whether it's choosing to befriend someone of another race, or asking a "nerd" or "jock" to help with homework, teenagers must learn to make choices that aren't shaped by stereotypes or racism.

LESSON AIM

To help senior highers learn how to confront the issues of stereotyping and racism.

OBJECTIVES

Students will:
● learn how tough it is to work with prejudiced people;
● explore how stereotypes hide who people really are;
● see how prejudices hinder Christ's message; and
● answer God's challenge to bring justice into their relationships.

BIBLE BASIS

ISAIAH 59:8-16a
ACTS 10:1-35

Look up the following scriptures. Then read the background paragraphs to see how the passages relate to your senior highers.

In **Isaiah 59:8-16a**, Isaiah paints a picture of oppression and injustice.

Injustice grieves God. He looks for someone who'll bring about justice—even to simply pray for justice. But in Isaiah's time, people who would cry out for justice were hard to find.

Teenagers can be challenged to answer God's call to right the wrongs of injustice. With God's help, teenagers can work to stop stereotyping and prejudice in their world.

In **Acts 10:1-35**, God confronts Peter's prejudices.

In Peter's day, it was unlawful for Jews to visit, or even associate with, anyone other than Jews. Peter, being a devout Jew, would've never associated with an unholy or unclean

Gentile. That is, until God revealed to Peter that all people are clean and precious to him.

Teenagers, like Peter, may be prejudiced against certain types of people based on race, age, social group or even grades. But by reading and understanding this passage, kids can learn the importance of every person—regardless of race, age or other categories that separate people.

THIS LESSON AT A GLANCE

Section	Minutes	What Students Will Do	Supplies
Opener (Option 1)	5 to 10	**Can't Judge a Book**—See how people can't be judged by their outward appearances.	Construction paper, markers, books
(Option 2)		**Stereotyping Clumps**—Experience how it feels to be stereotyped.	Paper, marker, tape
Action and Reflection	15 to 20	**Universal Prejudice**—Role play prejudiced aliens trying to work together.	"Solar Stereotypes" hand-out sections (p. 45), newsprint, marker, tape
Bible Application	10 to 15	**Arise and Eat**—Learn why people are prejudiced and how God can change prejudices.	Bibles, bread, pipe-cleaners
Commitment	5 to 10	**Changed Hearts**—Commit to accept God's challenge to fight injustice.	"New Hope" handouts (p. 44), pipe-cleaner shapes from Arise and Eat
Closing (Option 1)	5 to 10	**Breakout!**—Work to break out of prejudice and stereotyping.	Yarn
(Option 2)		**Cradled in Love**—Receive encouragement to rise above prejudice and fight for equality.	

The Lesson

OPTION 1: CAN'T JUDGE A BOOK

Form teams of no more than four. Give teams each construction paper, markers and four books; any books will do. Have groups each create book covers for their books. Have kids hide their books while they work on their covers, so others can't see the titles.

Say: **Each book-cover design must include some aspect of the actual book contents. For example, if your book is about animals, you might draw a picture of a cat or dog on the cover. You may not use any words on your covers.**

OPENER
(5 to 10 minutes)

Quickly look at your books to determine the content so you'll know what to depict on the covers.

Have groups each create their covers and then cover the books. One at a time, have groups present their books to the rest of the class. Have class members guess the title and contents of each book by its cover. After kids guess for each book, have the presenting group reveal the actual book title and its contents.

When all groups have presented their books, ask:

● **Was it easy to judge the contents of these books by the covers? Why or why not?** (Yes, the covers had enough information to help me make a good guess; no, there wasn't enough information.)

● **What does the phrase "You can't judge a book by its cover" mean?** (You can't assume things are what they seem; sometimes things are different on the inside than what they look like on the outside.)

● **How is trying to decipher the contents of these books by looking at their covers like guessing people's personalities based on their looks?** (You don't really know from the outside what people are like on the inside; you can make mistakes when you judge people by outward things.)

Say: **Judging people by outward appearance is a form of prejudice. Today we're going to explore how stereotyping, racism and other forms of prejudice can hurt people—and what we can do about it. And we'll each examine how we can get rid of our own prejudices.**

☐ OPTION 2: STEREOTYPING CLUMPS

Gather enough sheets of paper for each person in your room to have one. On each sheet of paper, write one of the following words: nerd, jock, punk, cheerleader, brain. You may have more than one sheet of paper with the same word. When kids arrive, tape one paper to each person's back. Don't allow kids to see the words on their own backs.

Say: **Walk around the room and say stereotypical things to or about people based on the categories written on their backs. For example, you might walk up to a "nerd" and say "Where's your pocket protector?" Or you might walk up to a "jock" and say "So . . . been working out lately?" You may make negative or positive comments, but they must be stereotypical. Don't tell people what their categories are. And don't be crude or cruel with your comments.**

Tell kids to look for people who are receiving the same kind of comments they are. After three minutes, call time and ask kids to each guess their stereotype. Then have them each look at their paper.

Ask:

● **How did you feel about the way people treated you? Explain.** (Angry, I didn't like being picked on; it didn't bother me, I'm not concerned about what others say.)

● **How do you think people feel when others categorize them by making comments similar to the ones you used?** (Upset; angry; hurt.)

● **Are stereotypes bad? Why or why not?** (Yes, they limit your friendships; no, they help you understand people.)

Say: **Stereotyping, like that we just experienced, is a form of prejudice. Today we're going to explore ways to fight stereotyping, racism and other forms of prejudice. And we're going to examine our own lives to see if we need to overcome prejudice.**

UNIVERSAL PREJUDICE

Photocopy and cut apart the "Solar Stereotypes" handout (p. 45). Form four groups. A group can be one person. Assign each group one of the following roles: Martians, Jupiterians, Saturnians or Mercurians. Give each group the corresponding handout section.

Say: **You've been invited to plan a party to honor Earthlings. In your group, read your role, and talk about how you'll act when you begin party-planning. Follow the instructions, and ham it up during the discussion time.**

Give kids three minutes to talk about their strategies. Have groups each come up with a "greeting" they'll use to begin the discussion; for example, a rhyme about their planet or beliefs.

While kids are planning, write the following actions on newsprint: (1) Determine who'll be note-taker; (2) Elect a party chairperson; (3) Decide on a menu; (4) Prepare seating arrangements; (5) Determine entertainment; and (6) Choose who'll say the opening prayer and what it'll be. Tape the newsprint to the wall.

Have kids sit in a square, with each group making up one side of the square. Have groups each present their greeting. Then say: **You're here today to plan a party for your favorite people—the Earthlings. You want the best party possible for your friends. The items on the newsprint represent some of the things you'll need to discuss to plan the party. You have six minutes to plan the party. Ready? Go.**

Remind groups to stay in character during this activity. After six minutes, or less if the discussion dies down earlier, call time. Have the chairperson explain what was decided.

Ask:

● **How easy was it to get things accomplished in this activity? Explain.** (Very difficult, people didn't communicate well; impossible, the other groups wouldn't listen to us.)

● **How did you feel about the way you were treated by other groups?** (It wasn't fair; I was angry; upset.)

● **How is that like the way people feel when others show prejudice against them?** (It's the same feeling; it's more painful in real life.)

● **How did your prejudices help or hurt the planning process?** (They hurt the process by stalling discussion; they helped by eliminating groups who didn't have much to offer.)

● **What does this activity tell us about prejudice?** (Prejudice makes people feel bad; prejudice keeps people from accomplishing tasks; it's easy to be prejudiced.)

Say: **Though you've probably heard about the civil rights movement of the '60s and the ongoing problems with racism around the world, you may not know prejudice existed even in Bible times.**

ARISE AND EAT

Read aloud Isaiah 59:8-16a and Micah 6:8.

Ask:

● **How does God view injustice?** (He hates it; he wants it abolished.)

● **How is prejudice a form of injustice?** (It limits people's freedoms; it hurts people needlessly.)

Have volunteers read aloud Acts 10:1-35. Form groups of no more than five.

Ask:

● **What did Peter learn in this story?** (God loves each person regardless of culture, race or creed.)

● **How did God change Peter's prejudice?** (By teaching Peter that all people are important.)

● **How are people today prejudiced against the following groups of people: women? homosexuals? Christian or other religious groups? activists for other causes?**

● **Why are people prejudiced today?** (They're uninformed; they're stupid; their parents were.)

Form pairs. Give each pair a piece of bread. Say: **This bread represents the walls of prejudice. By not eating this bread, we're upholding the traditions and ignorance that keep our prejudices intact. Like Peter, we're following the "rules" someone else set up that make us narrow-minded. Take turns with your partner holding the bread and telling one way you've acted unfairly toward someone. It might be as simple as giggling silently about the way someone was dressed, or telling ethnic jokes. Then talk about how you felt when you showed prejudice, or how you feel when others are prejudiced against you.**

Allow a few minutes for partners to tell each other their experiences. Then say: **Now both partners hold your piece of bread and slowly tear it in half. Then eat your half of the bread, or at least a small part of it. Say a silent prayer, asking God to break down the walls of prejudice so you can see that each person is loved by God.**

Give kids each a pipe-cleaner. Have them each silently form the pipe-cleaner into a symbol of the prejudice they've shown to someone else. Have volunteers tell what their pipe-cleaners represent, but don't force kids to talk about their symbols.

CHANGED HEARTS

Give kids each a "New Hope" handout (p. 44). Form a circle and have kids join you in the choral reading.

After the reading, have kids each re-shape their pipe-cleaner to symbolize how God can change people's attitudes toward others and give them strength to fight prejudice.

Have kids connect their pipe-cleaners together to form one large sculpture. Hang the sculpture in your meeting room as a reminder to treat people fairly.

☐ OPTION 1: BREAKOUT!

Have kids crowd together as tightly as possible. Help kids wind a ball of yarn around and through the group until kids are completely entangled in the yarn.

Ask:

● **How does prejudice entangle us and restrict us?** (It keeps us from making new friends; it gets us into trouble; it keeps us from reaching out to people in need.)

Say: **Peter learned from God that all people are important. When we learn that same lesson, we'll break out of the tangle of stereotyping and racism.**

Say one thing about each person in the group that might help that person break out of the restrictions of prejudice. For example, you might say: **(Name) can break out of the entanglements of prejudice because he's so caring.** Then have kids help you get that person out of the web of yarn. When all kids are untangled, hold hands in a circle. Close in prayer, asking God to help you treat other people with respect.

☐ OPTION 2: CRADLED IN LOVE

Form groups of three. Have two kids in each group stand side by side and lock arms to form a "cradle" for the third person to lean against. See the picture in the margin. Have the third person stand stiffly in front of the cradle, then gently lean back so he or she's held up by the other partners. Tell kids not to lean too far back.

While kids are cradled by their partners, have partners each tell the cradled partner one reason he or she can successfully rise above stereotyping or fight against prejudice. For example, someone might say: "Your kindness will help you open up to all people" or "Your love for God will help you know how to fight prejudice." Have kids each take a turn being cradled by their partners.

Form a circle and say: **With God's help, and support from each other, we can successfully defeat prejudice in our own lives and around the world.**

Close with prayer, thanking God for loving each person.

If You Still Have Time . . .

School Stereotypes—Form groups of no more than five. Have groups each choose one clique they know of to pantomime for the rest of the class. After each pantomime, have kids guess the clique and discuss how cliques promote stereotyping and prejudice. Have kids brainstorm ways to avoid cliques at their schools.

Course Reflection—Form a circle. Ask students to reflect on the past four lessons. Have them take turns completing the following sentences:

- Something I learned in this course was . . .
- If I could tell my friends about this course, I'd say . . .
- Something I'll do differently because of this course is . . .

NEW HOPE

Girls:	We don't know the way of peace.
Guys:	There's no justice in our tracks.
All:	Justice is far from us.
Girls:	We hope for light, but darkness prevails.
Guys:	We hope for brightness, but we walk in gloom.
All:	We grope along the wall like blind people.
Girls:	We grope like people who have no eyes.
Guys:	We stumble in daylight as if it were night.
All:	Among the strong, we're like dead men and women.
Girls:	We hope for justice.
Guys:	But there is none.
All:	Our prejudice keeps us from loving others.
Girls:	We turn away from people in need.
Guys:	And turn away from God at the same time.
All:	Yet there is a new hope. With God's help ...
Girls:	We can overcome our own prejudices.
Guys:	And challenge the racism and stereotyping we see around us.
All:	We can reach out and show God's love to all people.
Girls:	And be God's new hope for a world free from prejudice.
Guys:	God give us the strength to do your work.
All:	Amen.

Adapted from Isaiah 59:8-16a.

SOLAR STEREOTYPES

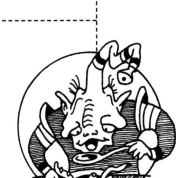

Martians:
- You tolerate the Saturnians, but you think all other aliens are "dweebs."
- You detest the Jupiterians because they love monga soup.
- You'd rather fight than be forced to eat monga soup.
- You pray to the Big Dipper.
- You think Mercurians only like mugbugli music.
- You know you're the best leaders for this committee because you're smarter than everyone else.
- You'd never lower yourselves to be note-takers for this meeting.

Jupiterians:
- You know you're superior to all other races.
- You'd rather not be at this meeting.
- You know you'd plan a better party without all these "glunks" "glurbs" and "gimlets" (Jupiterian slang for "idiots").
- You love to eat monga soup, and you plan to suggest it for the main course.
- You pray to the Big Dipper.
- You think Martians only like bamboomboom music.
- You wouldn't be caught dead taking notes—that's for low-lifes such as the Mercurians or Saturnians.

Saturnians:
- You know you're better than Jupiterians, but you respect the other alien groups.
- You love to eat fried cadbingle, and you plan to suggest it for the main course.
- You think your underwater barbershop quartet would make wonderful entertainment for the party.
- You'll reluctantly be note-takers for the meeting, but you'd rather lead the meeting.
- You think Martians don't know how to read or write.
- You pray to the Little Dipper.
- You think Mercurians only like tinwhallopy music.

Mercurians:
- You know you're superior to Martians and Jupiterians.
- You tolerate Saturnians, except for their love of fried cadbingle, which you think tastes like soggy wallpaper.
- You hope the other groups don't suggest music for the entertainment, because you detest all music.
- You don't want to take notes because you'd get your tentacles dirty.
- You're sure the Martians and Jupiterians are conspiring to take over your planet.
- You pray to the Big Dipper.
- You believe monga soup is only for weaklings; you'd rather have a smerg steak any day.

BONUS IDEAS

Justice System—Get permission to take your kids to a jury trial. Ask kids to observe how the lawyers attempt to protect people's rights. Afterward, have an attorney or a judge answer any general questions kids have about the legal system and personal rights.

Third-World Day—Contact one of the following organizations to get a program for a Third World Day for your class: World Vision ("The Planned Famine" program), Box O, Pasadena, CA 91109; or World Concern ("Refugee Camp" program), 19303 Fremont Ave. N., Seattle, WA 98133. After the event, have kids discuss ways they can reach out to people less fortunate than themselves.

Injustice Report—Assign kids or groups each a different country of the world to learn about. Have kids research their country and keep track of issues and events relating to justice in that country. Have kids or groups each report on their country once a month and offer specific prayers for their country during prayer time.

Injustice Fund-Raiser—Help kids choose a cause they'd like to raise money to support. Then have kids design fund-raising programs to collect money for and raise awareness of that situation. Check out *Fund Raisers That Work* by Margaret Hinchey (Group) for fund-raising ideas.

The Right to Discuss—Hold discussions on the issues of freedom of speech, equality and personal rights.
   Discuss:
   ● Does freedom of speech have a limit? If so, what is it?
   ● Is it right for a person less qualified than someone else to get a job because of his or her disability, race or sex—because a quota needs to be met? Why or why not?
   ● Is it fair for criminals to be set free because their rights were violated as they were being processed through the legal system? Why or why not?

Right the Wrongs—Have kids think of something they could do as a group to change an injustice. For example, they could sponsor a child together through Compassion International (Box 7000, Colorado Springs, CO 80933). Or they might help renovate or build homes for disadvantaged people through Group Workcamps (Box 599, Loveland, CO 80539) or Habitat for Humanity (419 W. Church St., Americus, GA 31709).

Table Talk—Use the Table Talk handout (p. 20) as the basis for a meeting with parents and teenagers. During the meeting, have parents and kids follow the instructions on the handout and discuss it together. Consider using this meeting as a fifth-week option to extend the curriculum course. Have kids assist you in presenting one or more of the activities from the four lessons to parents to help them "get into" the issues. Then have small groups parents and teenagers talk about injustice and choose things they can do to fight it.

Food and Stuff Collection—Use the " 'We Care' Scavenger Hunt" handout (p. 48) to send kids off on a scavenger hunt. Give groups of kids each a photocopy of the handout and see which team collects all the items first. Then go with kids to take the items to a local distribution center for helping poor or homeless people in your community.

Food for Thought—Plan a party to give kids a "taste" of what it's like to be poor or disadvantaged. During the party, serve simple foods such as crackers and water. Decorate the room with used decorations.

Kids may be disappointed with the food and decorations, but don't let them be disappointed with the games. Plan fun games and activities that don't require expensive props. Check out *Quick Crowdbreakers and Games for Youth Groups* (Group) for ideas. Then after the party, have kids talk about how injustices in the world can limit material things—but not the joy of being God's children. Have kids brainstorm ways to spread Jesus' message to people who are victims of injustice.

Unfair Retreat—Plan a retreat for kids to experience injustice. During the retreat, have kids participate in role-plays to see what it's like to go without food or shelter. Have kids skip a meal during the retreat. For another activity, have kids imagine they're survivors of a hurricane or earthquake. Give kids experiences to help them feel what it might be like to be victims of all kinds of injustice. Then spend the last day of the retreat discussing how kids felt and helping kids see how they can respond to injustice. Use Matthew 25:31-46 as the basis for a Bible study during the retreat.

PARTY PLEASER

RETREAT IDEA

"WE CARE" SCAVENGER HUNT

Work as a team to find the following items. You may get only one item from any one place you visit. Be sure to get donors' signatures and tell them what will be done with the donated items. The first team to return with all the items is the winner.

Item	Donor
1 can of green beans	_____
1 box of macaroni and cheese	_____
1 package of rice	_____
1 package of spaghetti	_____
1 jar of spaghetti sauce	_____
1 can of fruit (any kind)	_____
2 rolls of toilet paper	_____
1 can of corn	_____
1 jar of applesauce	_____
1 box of cereal (any kind)	_____
1 unopened tube of toothpaste	_____
1 unopened bar of soap	_____
1 can of tuna	_____
1 jar of any food item	_____
1 can of any food item	_____
1 box of any food item	_____